THE KATHLEEN PARTRIDGE SERIES

Kathleen Partridge's Book of Flowers
Kathleen Partridge's Book of Friendship
Kathleen Partridge's Book of Golden Thoughts
Kathleen Partridge's Book of Tranquil Moments
Kathleen Partridge's Book of Faith
Kathleen Partridge's Book of Happiness
Kathleen Partridge's Book of Seasons
Kathleen Partridge's Book of Hope

First published in Great Britain in 1997 by
Jarrold Publishing Ltd
Whitefriars, Norwich NR3 1TR

Designed and produced by Visual Image, Craigend, Brimley Hill,
Churchstanton, Taunton, Somerset TA3 7QH

Illustrations by Jane Watkins

Edited by Donald Greig

ISBN 0-7117-0970-X

Printed by Proost, Belgium 1/97

Kathleen Partridge's
BOOK OF
Faith

Kathleen Partridge

Somebody's Garden

Someone planned this garden
From the beauty in his soul
And kept his spirits joyful
As he worked towards this goal.

Breathing sunshine from the flowers
And wisdom from the leaves
To offer comfort to the sad
And peace to the heart that grieves.

From Heaven to Earth

The sunbeams dance down from a shaft out of
heaven
The perfume soars up where the lark sweetly sings
And that's why these flowers wear celestial colours,
The delicate texture of angels' wings.

And deep in the heart of the sweet passion flower
The stamens are formed as the calvary cross
Stained by the blood of our Lord's crown of thorns,
Marked by the tears that were shed for His loss.

Sleep Tight

In between the dimpled hills
Along a leafy lane
A pretty cottage slumbers
In the sunshine and the rain.

The roses ramble round it
Where the apple trees bend low
And good folk live in harmony
While fashions come and go.

The place where love is waiting
In the way that God designed,
When someone mentions 'Home'
This is the place that comes to mind.

Measure for Measure

The earth is the Lord's, I am His guest
His couch it is on which I rest,
His flock of birds sweet music trill
Upon my sunny windowsill.

His fields and hills my solace are
The morning dew, the evening star,
The fullness of the land and sea
These precious gifts He trusts with me.

Sunset

A golden shaft of sunlight
Makes a pathway to the sea
As if an angel host
Had walked into eternity

A blessing and a beauty
Never quite so fine before
That lights the sky at sunset
From horizon to the shore.

And then we know that God is good
Whatever man may do,
A sign of love shines up above
And hope is born anew.

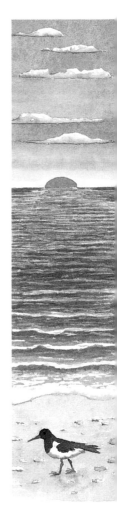

I Believe

Who can view the night and day
The sunset and the dawn
And yet deny Thy hand, Thy work,
Or treat one leaf with scorn?

Though men have many talents
For inventions here below,
Can man design one blade of grass
And make that blade to grow?

A spider's web, so frail a thing,
Yet in the morning dew
Can shine forth like a diadem
And bear the weight of dew.

Who can trap a snowflake
Or grow a flower from seed
And doubt the Lord will not be near
To help us in our need?

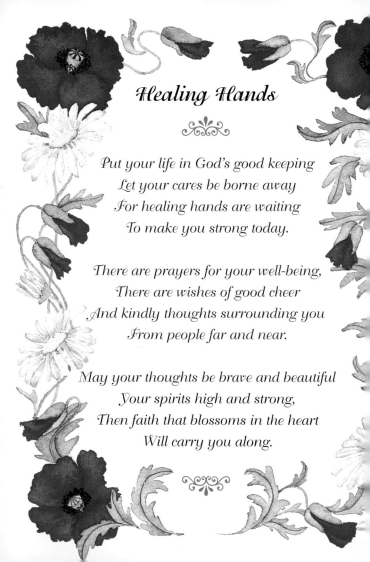

Healing Hands

Put your life in God's good keeping
Let your cares be borne away
For healing hands are waiting
To make you strong today.

There are prayers for your well-being,
There are wishes of good cheer
And kindly thoughts surrounding you
From people far and near.

May your thoughts be brave and beautiful
Your spirits high and strong,
Then faith that blossoms in the heart
Will carry you along.

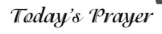

Today's Prayer

These are the things for which to pray:
Sufficient strength to meet the day;

Sufficient heart to cope with cares
And snags that take us unawares;

Sufficient patience to be found
To keep the peace with those around;

A sense of humour all day long
To turn a sigh into a song;

Sufficient joy of life and health
To live with zest, if lacking wealth;

Eyes that see the inner grace,
The beauty in the commonplace.

A Child's Prayer

Jesus, I bring my day to you
Each night when I have lived it through,
To show You how I am progressing
And ask You for Your kindly blessing.
Jesus, I bring my faults as well
And of my tempers, too, I tell
And ask Your pardon every night
For hopes too selfish to be right.
Jesus, here is my day's routine,
Correct the faults and wash it clean,
And give me, please, when these are gone
A new day to begin upon.

A Fresh Start

May God wipe out our failures
As the night blacks out the day
And while we sleep fold up our cares
And send our fears away.

Thus every day we start afresh
Upon a spotless page,
This is the morning gift of God
Our earthly heritage

St Christopher

St Christopher, the kind and strong,
Who helped a little child along
And found he'd saved the world from harm
By lending Christ his valiant arm.

St Christopher, with the Messiah,
Guard the motorist and the flyer;
The big ship and the fisher boat,
The infant with the toy to float.

St Christopher, the traveller's friend,
Protect our journey to the end,
And, by example, make us strong
To help our fellow men along.

Lend us your courage and your smile
To tread in faith the extra mile,
To find our cheerful ways sufficed
To lift the world by helping Christ.

Hope

Reach out and cling to hope when the
demand for it arises,
For it's hope that keeps us smiling when
our ship of dreams capsizes;
And hope that puts a timely finger on
our sinking chin –
That brings a light into the darkness
when despair creeps in.

A fragile thread, a tiny flame, a spark
however small,
A beam of hope that waits close by to be
within our call.
For hope has lifted many lives and saved
great hearts from sinking,
It is a lifeline to the mind engrossed with
saddened thinking.

Silent Prayers

Receive my silence, Lord,
When I am lost for words to pray
Look deep into my heart
And read the words I cannot say.

I long to tell my fears
But daren't, in case I fear anew,
In silence and humility
I bring my cares to You.

Hear me, help me, love me
Because You know I care,
And in my silence read
A feeble, but fervent prayer.

Watch for the Dawn

Watch for the dawn to lift your fighting power,
Wait for the light to change the darkest hour
Suffering is borne by holding on and hoping,
Daring to live by keeping on and coping.

You, even you, are braver than you know
And stronger than you think, when progress is slow
Watch for the dawn throughout the darkest night
And join the birds singing with the morning light.

Turn of the Tide

Brave heart, brave spirit, you will battle through
To good health and horizons that are new;
Look straight ahead and deal not with dismay
The light is there to guide you on your way.

Let faith be yours to face what is to be
The tide will turn upon the darkest sea,
Brave heart, brave spirit with a gentle soul,
God hear our prayers, and hearing make you whole.

Harvest

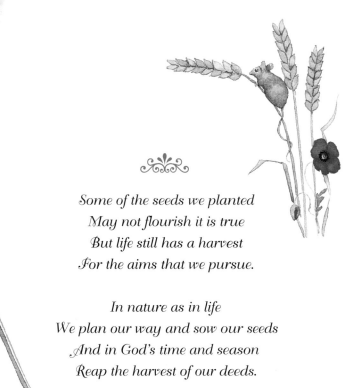

Some of the seeds we planted
May not flourish it is true
But life still has a harvest
For the aims that we pursue.

In nature as in life
We plan our way and sow our seeds
And in God's time and season
Reap the harvest of our deeds.

Life is a Prayer

What fitter prayer could be designed
Than little actions that are kind!
Is there a better living creed
Than sympathy in time of need?

What greater psalm or hymn of praise
Than cheerfulness and courteous ways
For who can love the Lord God when
He loves not first his fellow men?

Sail On

There is a port to which our aims are sailing,
Where disillusion and discord are shed,
A harbour where each heart will find its anchor
Somewhere in the years that lie ahead.
There may be storms to face before we find it
And tattered sails to be retrimmed and set,
Some find it quickly, some still dream about it
And others haven't recognised it yet.
But there's a port, a place for every person,
Philosophy makes every sea grow calm,
Where bold adventure loses its excitement
And quiet days and twilights have more charm.
Sail on, brave ships, towards your little heavens,
Gather your wisdom as you go on your way,
Trust in your stars and keep your compass steady
And follow your fate into a peaceful bay.

Looking Ahead

May you see beyond the grimy buildings
To all the glory of the highest hill,
May you look beyond the cares of living
To where the promised joy is shining still.

May you see between the narrow roadways
To all the clover growing in the green,
Heeding not the turmoil of existence
Because a blackbird sings above the scene.